Dedicated to

Sonic The Hedgehog (Sonic 06) on the Xbox 360. If you hadn't been the absolute hot mess you turned out to be, I may never had made the first episode of The Sonic Show.

The Sonic Show and The Sonic Show's Book of Almost
Everything Copyright © 2015 by Jame Egge Mann.
Sonic the Hedgehog is copyright © SEGA Corporation.
This book and it's contents is in no way associated by
SEGA Corporation.
All rights reserved.
No part of this publication may be reproduced,
distributed, or transmitted in any form or by any means,
including photocopying, recording, or other electronic or
mechanical methods, without the prior written
permission of the publisher or author, except in the case
of brief quotations embodied in critical reviews and
certain other noncommercial uses permitted by
copyright law.

First Edition, 2015
thesonicshow.org
youtube.com/thesonicshow
twitter.com/sonic_show

WELCOME TO THIS MESS OF WORDS.

The story of how The Sonic Show started is an interesting one going back many years. So it's a great shame that nobody here can be bothered to tell it. In fact, The Sonic Show has always been quite lazy in archiving its history and sharing any insight.

We decided however, that we needed to do something. So join us through this book as we cover our show's history, the people who made it, and our favourite highlights. Presented to you in a glorious, badly written and lazy fashion. And don't worry, there are pictures too.

THE BEGINNING.

I have been a fan of Sonic since, well, forever. My first games console was a Sega Mega Drive, which came along with the spin off title Sonic Spinball. I fell in love, and that was before I even saw Sonic 2. That **blew** my mind as a child. As with all kids my age, as soon as we got hold of the internet, I quickly found a home to share my obsessive fascination with the blue blur.

For me, it was The Sonic Stadium. A site with ambitious visions. It covered news, had a popular message board, its own Sonic themed video show and online radio station. It was like my home. Logging in daily to talk to my friends, thinking the site owner Dreadknux was so cool, I was such an addict. I listened to their radio shows religiously, I wanted them to make a podcast so bad. Little did I know that years later I would be doing just that for them.

As I mentioned, they also had their own video show which was known as Sega Sonic : TV. I posted on the forum that I found the quality rather lacking. Possibly a bit harsh, but while I enjoyed it, I did find some issues with what they were doing. Clearly my thoughts weren't that well received as another forum member named, "Zizou" told me that, "If you think you can do better, go on then."

So I did.

And so, The Sonic Show was a thing. Yay.

A banner I made for the message boards of The Sonic Stadium. If only I knew I'd be doing a podcast on this very site.

THE VIDCAST YEARS

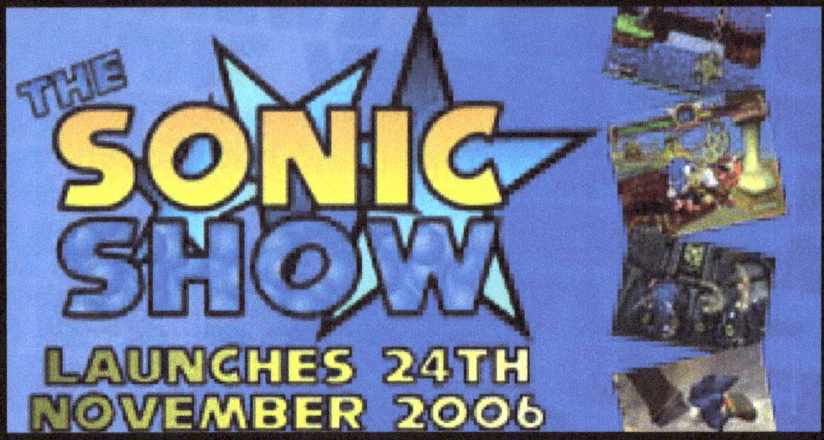

The first episode of The Sonic Show was, and forever will be, a complete mess.

I didn't have a camera of any kind to record myself hosting the show. So instead, I created a looping video featuring video clips from Sonic games scrolling past the screen. Then, with a crappy microphone I recorded my narration over this footage. It wasn't the best approach, but it did the job. The first segment of the video was an AMV (internet term for clips of something played along to a song). Not only is an AMV now considered one of the most fan-boyish types of content on the internet, it was a Sonic X AMV. What was I thinking? The whole pilot episode was wrapped up with a regular segment where I would battle my sister at a Sonic game. And what did we do for the first episode? Sonic The Fighters. It was... not good. We never did that "regular" segment again.

I don't hate all of the first episode. You have to remember I was a teenager who had never done anything like this before, so it was never going to be a masterpiece. I think what I liked about this first episode the most was how I made a whole piece on how broken the Gameboy Advance port of Sonic The Hedgehog was. It was that desire to openly accept and poke fun at the flaws in the franchise that set the tone of the show for rest of its life.

YouTube wasn't really a thing in 2006. It was still very new and wasn't the mammoth being it is today. However, there was one hugely popular media format booming back then, and that was podcasting. By uploading my videos in a 320x240 resolution to a server and creating an RSS feed, I was able to submit my content to the growing podcast section on the extremely popular iTunes store. Kids and teenagers across the world all had these fancy new iPods and as we were the first to do it, we were the first result when searching the iTunes store for Sonic The Hedgehog.

I'm not sure why it took off so quickly. I can only imagine that a large part of it had to do with the fact that there was only one other video format entertainment show for Sonic. Everyone was doing fan radio or ran fan sites with written content. The only other video show online (SEGASonic:TV) was only viewable from their website page, so lost out on the accessibility our audience had of downloading episodes easily and taking them on the road on their portable players.

I quickly realised I hated the sound of my voice, so took on three people to present the show while I simply wrote the script and edited the overall episode. After some searching I found Todd, Andy and Saph, and together we made an awesome team.

With my show only continuing to grow, I was contacted during the production of the third episode by Zizou. It turns out the person who had a go at me for critiquing the show that inspired me to do my own, was the owner of Sonic Cage Dome. SCD was a huge fan site featuring a wide network of creative people and they wanted The Sonic Show on their roster. Without much hesitation I accepted and moved the show to their network, where we lived happily for our first season's full run of 10 episodes.

They helped propel us into the conscious of the Sonic community. And for that I will always be grateful.

SCD PRESENTS

THE SONIC SHOW

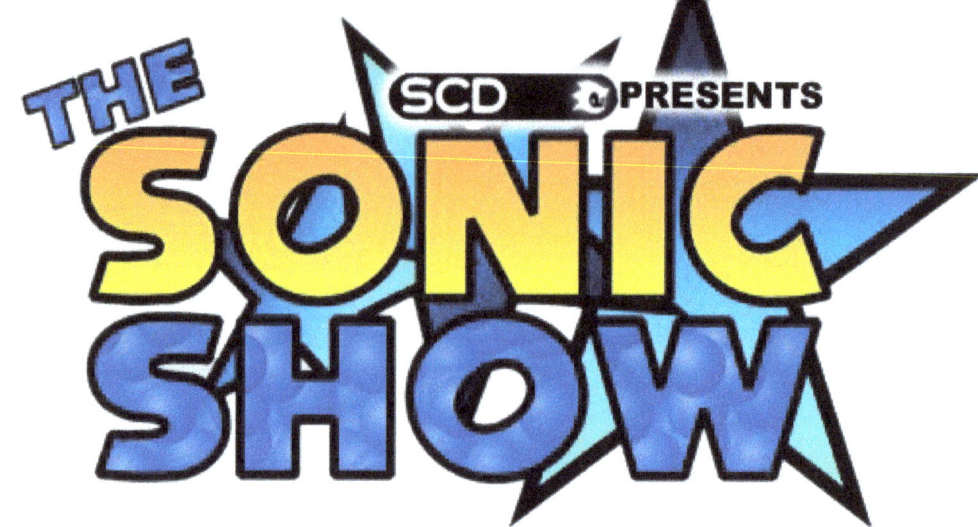

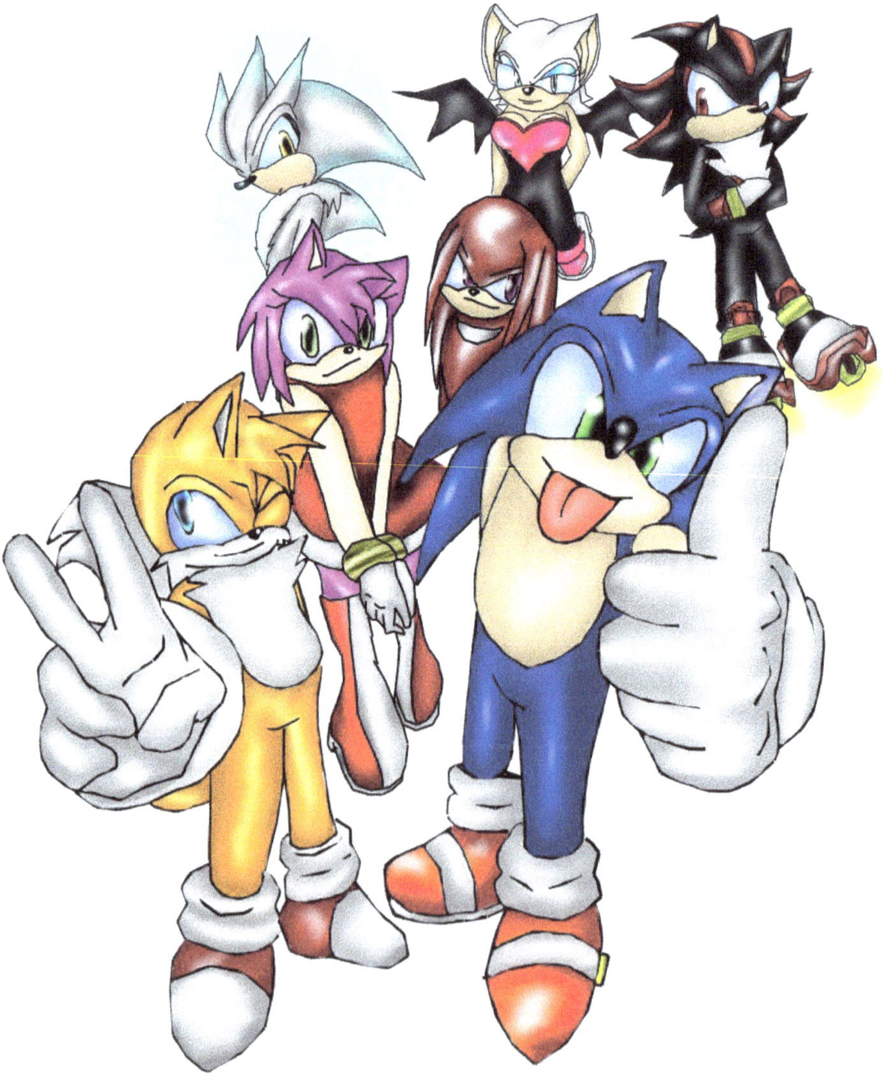

THE CHATTY BIT

Brent Johnston aka Todd Hakusho
Show Host 2006-2008

You were the first ever member of the crew Jay took on. How did you get involved in the show.
Well, from what I can recall, There was either a casting call in a message board thread about hosting this new "Sonic Show". I - being a fan of Sonic and a member of TSS at the time - figured it'd be fun, not ever expecting I'd be chosen out of all who showed interest. Still don't know how I managed that (chuckle).

The show was very different at the start, what was the process of making an average episode.
Back in the day, Jamie would send me a script....which was a single/ two pages of collective lines for me to say. I recorded them - looking back, I wish I had better equipment but I digress - and email him the finished audio files. I'd then see the final product upon its release.

The Sonic Show is a different beast these days, what are your thoughts on it's growth and do you ever miss the "gold old days"?
To be honest, I feel that, perhaps, the change was for the best; the show was experiencing growing pains and cramming all the news and content it now shows into monthly episodes would have been a disaster waiting to happen.
...that said, do I miss working for it? Hell yes! It was a fun time and I would give anything if I had the chance to host it again! Good times man, good times.

You weren't the only host after the first few episodes. What are your memories of your co hosts Andy and Saph
Sadly, Andy and I never truly hit it off; don't get me wrong, he was a nice guy, we just never really talked much outside of the show, if I recall correctly. I haven't heard a peep from him since least 2007.
As for Saph, the one memory I have regarding her was the day we started what has become a strong friendship. It was a few months or so after her house had burned down, and I had decided to send an email to get her MSN...I figured since she was a member of the show, why not get contact info?
Well after her and I exchanged info, we ended up chatting into the wee hours of that same day. Thankful to the show for that; she's become one of my best friends.

That was all 6 years ago, are you surprised the show is still going?
I am actually not surprised that the show has still been going. As long as Sonic keeps running strong, so will the show. So long as the fan community contributes to the fandom, the show will showcase it. Kind of inspiring how it's come from an idea to what it is now, huh?

A QUICK LOOK AT SEASON ONE

Even in our first year we created holiday specials.

In our 7th episode collaboration with Radio Redux, Wrecksfest took on the spirit of the opening of cheers.

In our second episode we showed off the amazing physics of Sonic 06.

Our first animation. Created by a chap named 'Auzzy'.

In our pilot Jay battled his sister in Sonic The Fighters.

A NEW SEASON, A NEW HOME

You could say that the vidcast years of The Sonic Show were our "Rock n' Roll" years. Well, a really underwhelming version of that anyway. One thing we did do well though was drama.

Towards the end of our first season of the show, I came into contact with Svend, a guy more commonly known as Dreadknux. He owned The Sonic Stadium, arguably one of the biggest fan sites on the internet. The Sonic Stadium was a big deal and Svend wanted The Sonic Show to be part of his armour. It was difficult to decide whether this was a move I should make. Sonic Cage Dome were like family and helped in major way to put our brand out there. But, to me, The Sonic Stadium was the holy grail of Sonic communities. To refuse it would have been a wrong move. I took the plunge and confirmed to Svend that I wanted to join his ranks. That was then followed by a very uncomfortable conversation with Zizou that our Season 1 finale episode would be our last at Sonic Cage Dome. While he never said anything bad to me, Zizou was very cold. It was clear he felt insulted. If that wasn't difficult enough, a lot of the fans close to the SCD website took it personally when we left. It wasn't an easy choice to move, but one that paid off in the end.

2008 saw the start of Season 2 at its new home on The Sonic Stadium. Things were bigger and better; episodes were even longer in length, we had guest presenters, plus our strongest line up of original content. Two of the biggest hitters were Slingerland's Corner and Red Hedgehog. The former, a harsh attack on the most obnoxious parts of fandom dressed up as an Agony Aunt section where fans could get advice from Brad the counselor. The latter, a comedic review of the tropes of Sonic games animated by the talented Evil Doc duo.

The show only got bigger and put its foot firmly in the door of community. Unfortunately, this would not last forever.

A QUICK LOOK AT SEASON TWO

The star of the controversial "Slingerland's Corner". The talented Brad.

The now infamous Evil The Hedgehog.

The Sonic Show was there for the first Summer Of Sonic. We have been part of the convention every year.

Season 2 saw some weird videos. Like this Girls Aloud song seen through the eyes of Amy Rose.

Season 2 saw us ask non Sonic fans what words meant in "Sonicisms". This is my mother.

THE CHATTY BIT
Svend Joscelyne
The Sonic Stadium Founder

What made you decide to invite The Sonic Show to your popular network back in 2008?

The Sonic Show represented a unique creativity within the Sonic fan base that hadn't yet been tapped - video. Nobody had really done video in a big way before - YouTubers were scattered all over the place with no big vision or idea. The Sonic Show was really the first time where a video show about Sonic had a direction and, in many ways, a purpose.
I was an avid fan of the first season and its episodic structure, offering a number of interesting and humourous content in one package. I wanted to bring the show under the TSS Network so that Jamie's passion and creativity could further evolve into what it is today

UNSEEN

Here is a sample of the concept logo and artwork for Season 2. Both were abandoned for the final blue logo (see left) and a more Sonic Channel inspired style artwork (see next page).

Season 2 Show Artwork

by Professor-J

professor-j.deviantart.com

THE YOUTUBE TRANSITION!

Making season two was a struggle. Creating a long format show required getting a lot of different people to work together and all on the same schedule. And as the show got bigger in scale, making all these different parts fit together became harder and harder to do. A whole episode could be basically done, but because one person hadn't done their bit, the whole thing could not go out to the public. With this in mind, the show's second season came to a halt after four episodes.

It was a dark time for the show, I was frustrated and didn't know if I had the motivation to continue producing these episodes. On top of that, the way people viewed content was changing. The first smart phones were becoming the norm. People could watch content on demand any time they wanted. People could instantly watch a five minute video between doing things without a moments thought. People didn't want to download an hour long video that would take forever to get onto their device. People wanted quick and simple content. It was a combination of this change in the way video was consumed and the difficulty in making long format videos that made me decide that the format of the show needed to change forever.

The season format was dead. Season two came to a sudden close and there would not be a season three in sight. From now on we would release smaller videos on a more regular basis. One video could be a review, the next one a comedy sketch. The important thing was we could release each idea as soon as it was done, rather than wait for a collection of other parts to be ready as well. Not only did we change the way we released videos but also where we released those videos. I had a personal Youtube account under my internet name, "Discoponies". This would be the new home for our videos, and the start of a new chapter for the show. With a brand new logo by Professor J, a new theme song by Hunter Bridges and a whole new intro animated by Josiah Haworth, things were looking up for the show's future.

2009 Logo
by Professor-J
professor-j.deviantart.com

2009 - 2012 Show Art
by Legend20x
legend20x.deviantart.com

Back when the show first started in 2006, I was not just following content created by The Sonic Stadium. I was also a huge fan of Radio Redux. This was a podcast hosted by ArchangelUK (better known now as Kevin Eva) on the Sonic Wrecks website. While we were growing to be the number one choice for Sonic vidcasts, Radio Redux was already the number one audio podcast for Sonic fanatics.

Not even two episodes into doing The Sonic Show, Kevin was the first person to give me a shout out on his show. In fact, Kevin has always been extremely supportive of my work throughout his time in the community. Not only was he hugely supportive of us through his podcast, but he even agreed to collaborate with us in a crossover episode. Mixing the styles and tones of both The Sonic Show and Radio Redux, it was a one of a kind episode that I am very proud of.

While Radio Redux and Sonic Wrecks are no longer around these days, Kevin is still going strong with his newest website Last Minute Continue. To this day he still works on crossover projects with us, including Sonic Boom Commentaries, a podcast/video show where he reviews and commentates on the Sonic Boom television show. I'm quite certain wherever The Sonic Show goes in the future, he will be there somewhere backing us!

The Sonic Show Website: A Timeline

The original website from November 2006.

A mere month later we moved to Sonic Cage Dome. Featuring a wonderful grey line in a highly buggy wordpress theme.

Jump to the start of 2007 and we refreshed the whole show's look.

Towards the end of 2007 we (for some reason) went with a very simple and modest look.

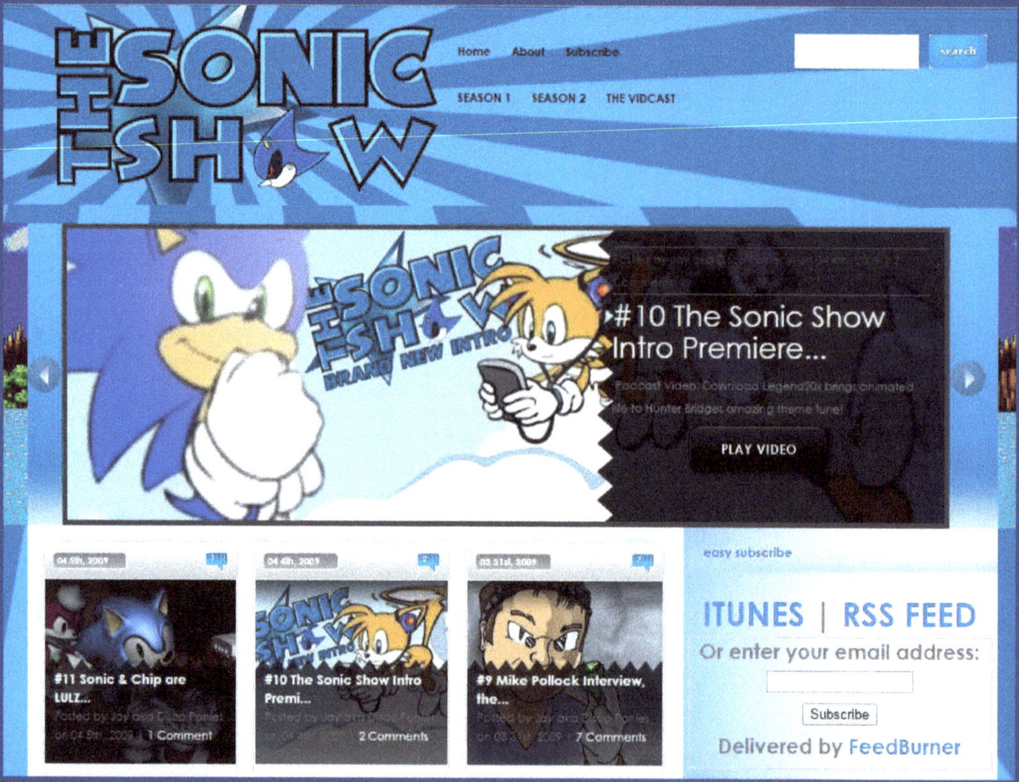

At The Sonic Stadium we dropped the season format and launched a whole new look and approach in 2009.

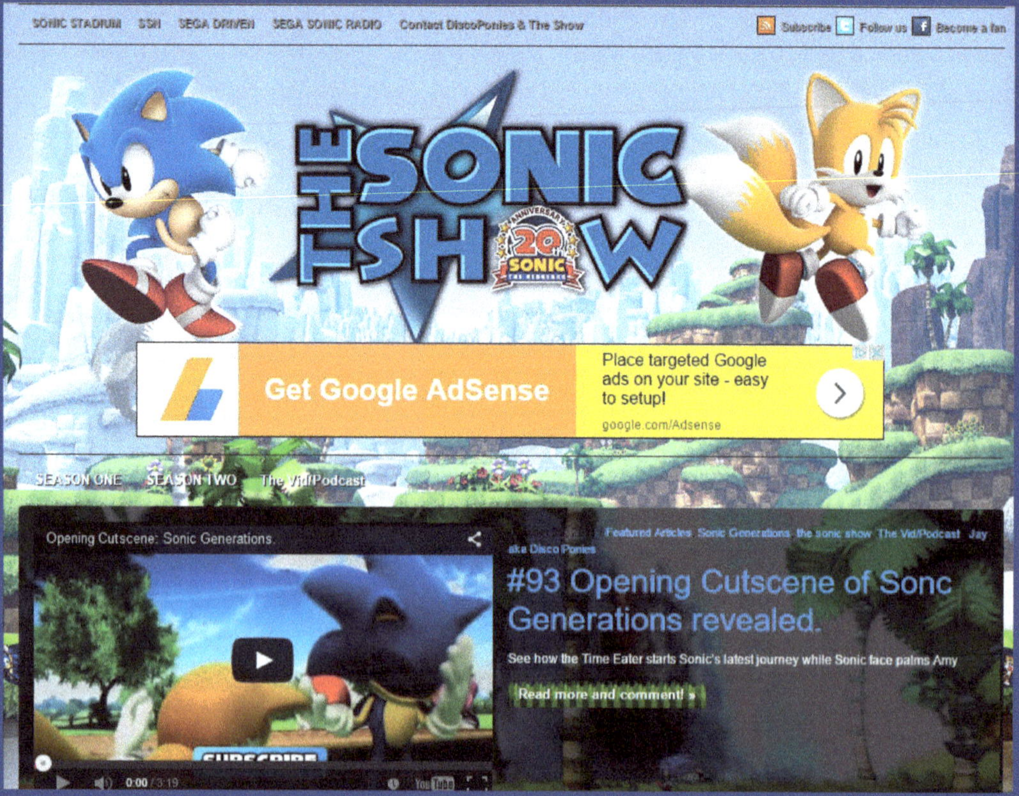

Of course it was impossible to avoid everything having a Sonic Generations flavour in 2011.

2012 saw the biggest relaunch in the show's history. That included a brand new website.

In 2014 we simplified the website into a explanation of what we created and information on the team.

THE NEW START.

August, 2011.

What a crap month.

We had just started hitting our stride on YouTube. Videos were picking up attention and it seemed like we found our new home. Well, that's what I thought.

I logged into my YouTube account that month to see our Youtube profile's customisation settings had been reset to default. Thinking it must have been a glitch, I simply set it all back. For some stupid reason that did not set my alarm bells ringing. I'll tell you what did though. Finding my password was changed and all our videos deleted. Great.

As you can imagine, I was a wreck. The deletion of my videos tied into a very recent crash of a hard drive that stored our content. Luckily, I had it all backed up on Youtube. Oh wait... bollocks. So yes, it was a huge kick in the chest for myself. However, what I wasn't prepared for was the outpouring of love from the community.

I knew I had to act fast on this. I couldn't look at it as an end, I had to use it as an opportunity to take advantage of. It was almost like a sign. I also had an unused Youtube account called "TheSonicShow" just laying there. I threw the artwork on it, uploaded a video explaining the hacking situation and watched not only the fans come back, but a whole new audience wanting to support too.

HELP US SHOW THIS TROLL THAT WE WONT STAND FOR HIS HACKING!

In a weird kind of way the loss of our channel was a blessing in disguise. It forced us to use a channel that had the URL of our actual name, not to mention the huge press it got helped bring eyes to our work. I would still love our old channel back of course. Who knows, maybe some of our forever lost videos are still sat there set as private. I guess we will never know. I'm sure that hacker felt they achieved something and I will never get the chance to say to them what I think of their antics. Though, if that hacker should ever read this, I have one thing to say to them.

I HOPE IT WAS WORTH IT FOR 300 SUBSCRIBERS AND NO VIEWS WHILE WE HAVE TENS OF THOUSANDS OF SUBSCRIBERS AND MILLIONS OF VIEWS. SUCK IT.

Or something like that.

So, a new channel and new start. This was a new era (again) for the show. Smartphones were now common place and people just weren't watching content on devices like iPods anymore. It was time to leave vidcasting behind.

Not only did I focus on Youtube as my primary focus of media, but I even started to explore new ventures too. The first was a weekly live stream, where I played a variety of classic Sonic games. I was absolutely terrible. I was so bad in fact that the "death counter" was a popular recurring feature. It was also during these streams that I started inviting random people into the broadcasts. Some of whom started to work on the main show itself and have been with me ever since! I will never forget people like Grace and BlueKirby for what they added to the live streams and I am glad doing those shows brought me to the likes of people such as Tanner, Fuad and Tom.

So yeah, in retrospect, I say thank you to that hacker. You may be a huge douche, but your award winning twattery only made The Sonic Show stronger.

THE CHATTY BIT
Tanner aka Goodbye18000
The Sonic Show resident Let's Player.

How did you first discover The Sonic Show?
A long, long time ago, in an era of iPods that just got video, I got a, well, iPod Video one year for Christmas. This led to me getting iTunes and downloading a bunch of stuff based on things I love. Now, I loved Sonic music so I looked for it on there. Sadly, it wasn't, but something free popped up instead – The Sonic Show. A podcast. I downloaded it because hey, it was free, and listened in. Needless to say, it was hilarious. I remember showing my friends Slingerland on the bus (I was in Grade 6 at the time) and listened to the Bentley Jones soundtrack sampler over and over. It was awesome.

You are now very much a regular in the show's cast. How did you get involved in the show?
I remember finding The Sonic Show's original Youtube channel one day when I was looking for an older video. I subscribed and enjoyed it, but then one day, the impossible happened. It got hacked. From there, The Sonic Show had to start from scratch with a new channel, and I was one of the first subscribers. From there, I showed my friend Fuad it, and when they held an audition for a Black Doom voice for a Halloween video, he got in contact with Jamie and became friends with him. Following that, I was asked by him if I wanted to join a Skype call with them. I basically died (I watched these guys as a kid and now I'm with them?!?) and joined in. Needless to say, it was amazing. From there, Jamie asked me if he could host the currently running Sonic 2 XL Let's Play that was on my channel on the official Sonic Show channel, to which I told him he could use anything for me and I would do anything for him. Boy, did that seal my fate, huh?

Which of your videos are you most proud of. And which do you have less fond memories of?
It's really hard to think about what I'm most "proud" of, cause I'm not really super proud of any of my videos. As a Let's Player, I put out frequent, low quality content. It's kind of our shtick. One exception I could say is my Top 10 Easter Egg in Sonic. While it was originally just a filler thing, it went on to get half a million views (as of now) and is the cause of many debates. I wish I put more time into it (like the audio mixing) but it went on to do wonders! The one I'm least proud of goes back to when I told Jamie I'd do anything for him. This one's a toss up between the stupid dance video – where I was called "fat" in the comments a lot and it actually hurt me a bit – and the Double Hedgehog if only for the legacy it left on me. I am a registered artist on Spotify AND MORE because of that.

Where do you see the future of The Sonic Show going?
The future of The Sonic Show is a tough one. On the one hand, Sonic's in this weird period where it doesn't know where it's going. Because of that, we honestly have a lot to talk about in our Opinion Zones, which will continue, and our commentaries on games and TV shows. I think we will continue to dig into the past while observe the present and future for the channel. Plus with the near daily discoveries of scraped Sonic games and media, we have so much to look forward to in the future even with the estranged present of the franchise.

2012 - Present Show Art
by Nick Kalmer
piggybank12.deviantart.com
(Logo by Professor-J.deviantart.com)

THE CHATTY BIT

Chris 'Crofty' Light

VGM:Awesome host and Red Panda Audio founder

You came across The Sonic Show thanks to cohost Jono D, what did you think of it?
To me The Sonic Show is the church of Sonic fans, bringing a crazy hodge podge of devoted fans and Sonic lovers from all corners of Mobius under one roof for the best of the land. I've seen that these community members are allowed to celebrate and express their love for Sonic characters and games without judgment and amongst like minded individuals. Now all bow to The Sonic Show!

You are part of Red Panda Audio, the team that brought the current theme music for the show, what is the creation process?
It's a two man setup, Matthew Walker and myself. The process in writing music is no different to anything else we forge. Matt slaps his messy musical brush all over the musical canvas, it's then left to me to arrange the slaps of musical colour into something that sounds non-offensive.

You've seen Jay play games first hand, is he really as bad as he makes out in his videos?
Yes, he is just awful. Once he didn't come last probably because he trained all week. I'm struggling to think of a game that is not remotely bad at...tick tack toe?
Is this enough?

THE CHATTY BIT

Matthew 'MattVV' Walker
VGM:Awesome host and Red Panda Audio founder

What are your observations of The Sonic Show?
The Sonic Show is a massive community of fans that not only get the chance to create, watch and amass their involvement but have the opportunity to share a common interest that otherwise wouldn't have been available to them so accessibly. The show & brand is packed full of quirky content that maintains a very particular style and humour, never once forgetting its source material.

The Sonic Show took part in your Sonic Off, how did it come about?
The 'Sonic-off' is the ultimate challenge between VGMA co-pres Jono D and any willing Sonic the Hedgehog fan to try their damnedest to shatter Sir D's throne as the ultimate Sonic fan. The idea came about after it became apparent during a VGMA show that JonoD simply had to challenge the founder of the Sonic Show after VGMA had formed a collaborative relationship with the show - it was a natural decision and progression to get the two together in a darkened room and shine a light on exactly what these guys know and more importantly don't know about Sonic the Hedgehog!

Red Panda Audio are the master minds behind the shows current theme music. What is the process behind that?
Red Panda Audio prides itself on its personal composition and mastering process. To begin with, it's important to gather as much inspiration as possible - this can come from all sorts of avenues - most importantly though, from the client themselves - what would they like to hear? What inspires them? As lead composer, I will dig deep into the musical & emotional needs of our client, finding out exactly their intended sound. Then spend many many many hours listening to music and dabbling with compositional ideas before writing the piece - this then gets forwarded onto Chris who will add his very different approach to composition to the piece, adding to the quality of the track and providing a different perspective. Piece then gets mastered, making sure that every frequency and instrument is balanced, maintaining that initial intended sound.
The reaction was great and Red Panda Audio is massively proud to have written something that the many Sonic Show fans feel is a theme worthy of the name.

You've seen Jay play games first hand, is he really as bad as he makes out in his videos.I think Jay has a lot of potential as a professional video gamer - his opinion that he is a bad player is a massive decoy, I believe the man spends crazy hours down his local underground 'VG Club' whereby he trains and battles, bare-chested, operating analog sticks with his ears.

SUMMER IS THE SEASON OF SONIC

One of the greatest things about doing The Sonic Show has been our involvement in Summer Of Sonic. Between 2008 and 2013, members of the community hosted a Sonic themed convention with the support of SEGA. The Sonic Show has been there every year to cover the event and live stream the events to the wider world. Through doing it I have made life long friends and met many of you guys who watch the show. It's truly a humbling experience when people who watch what you do come and speak to you. It is also a tiny bit weird, but that's just because I'm a complete introvert.

I have also had the pleasure of working at other Sonic events such as the rapidly growing Weston Super Sonic convention. Who knows what events we will venture to in the coming years!

I've have had many fun times working with the Summer Of Sonic gang, and while we may not have another one on the cards in the immediate future, I am sure that it won't take a lot to get the old band back together.

FANS SHARE THE LOVE...

AWESOME! ★★★★★
by JTGrimmfire – Feb 2, 2007
Any fan of Sonic or the others should suscribe to this podcast.It rocks!

NeoMetallix 1 year ago
Hi guys, great channel you have here! :) Keep up the good work.
Reply •

BPGameplayNet 4 years ago
Hey guys! This is a great channel! You do really high quality work and take me back to the 90s with some of your great videos, plus I mostly watch my Sonic Generations previews from you guys. Keep up the great work! Im a huge fan!

TheRealSonicFan 4 years ago
Awesome Channel dude. Subscribed ;)

Jesse aka FireGXLOL 3 years ago
I like what this channel is doin here

THIS IS MY FAVORITE VIDEO PODCAST! ★★★★★
by DJ Raddy - Mar 4, 2007
I love these videos just as much as I like video games (though i wish they create and post them faster). I hope they stay as one of the most popular podcasts. I just can't explain how awesome this podcast is! I watch the videos everyday!

guizml ♪♫ @Guizml · Sep 27
@sonic_show HI LOVE YOU SONIC SHOW :3
  1   3

Pure Awesomeness ★★★★★
by KeithUzumaki – Jan 21, 2007
I Love this podcast. I am only 13 and I have been around sonic my whole life. My Dad had a Genesis when I was 3. I would sit around and play all day.I really like this podcast. keep up the good work guys!!!

...AND THE HATE.

It stinks! ★☆☆☆☆
by Qwertyyuuioopashjkllhdaxcvn — Oct 19, 2010

Boo!

XxX_EATSTEEL_XxX EATMETAL 6 days ago
the sonic show? more like the sonic blows
Reply

Nicky The Fox 1 month ago
ive seen some weird stuff but this is just wow... what the fuck iiiiiissssss this shit?
Reply

ZippyZakGamer 2 years ago
You suck sorry but you can't hate an fan characters!

Spookata Skyshiro @SegaSky · 3m
.@sonic_show ur nasty and a bitch

CinosGaming 4 days ago
oh f*ck me
y
y
so u hate a f*cking video game just cuz fanart
u didnt even tell us wut is wrong with it
and its gr8 anyways so dont even try
if i could make a drinking game out of u i would now be stuck

Bam Hurger 17 hours ago
This is the worst thing ever and I hope Mega64 does a content claim or whatever to shut this hellhole down.

In 2014 we released a compilation album. Featuring our variety of original music going all the way back to the start of The Sonic Show, it was certainly a collector's item. Was it a musical master piece? Let me allow Sega Driven to answer that one for you.

> *"The parodies obviously have more appeal to the wider Sonic audience and while they're certainly amusing, they won't be something you revisit a lot and the vocal performances are more functional than anything you could call talented. Also there's a worrying amount of audio spikes that are pretty harsh on the ears... The Sonic Show's Complete Mess Collection is an aptly titled selection of music and parodies that doesn't have a wide appeal. It's a nice little item that fans of the show will want to own, but it's not a collection of music that the general Sonic fan will listen to more than once making this an awkward release to recommend."*
> *Written by Lewis "Sonic Yoda" Clark on 01/11/2014 SEGADRIVEN.COM*

As you can see, critically acclaimed hit.

What Does The Fox Say Lyrics:

Chao goes, Wisp goes.
Rouge goes, Shadow goes.
Jet goes. Amy goes, and Omochao goes.
Eggman says, Knuckles goes, and Sonic goes.
But there's one sound that no one knows...
WHAT DOES THAT FOX SAY?

Big blue eyes, high I.Q, first met him, in Sonic Two.
Fixes things, did you know , flies a plane called Tornado.
Your fur is soft, so beautiful, and you even have two tails.
But if I made you turn and roll, would I see there two bum ho-o-o-o-oles, ho-o-o-o-oles, ho-o-o-o-oles?
I'm sure that would be so-or-or-ore, so-or-or-ore, so-or-or-ore!
WHAT THAT FOX SAY?

The truth about you fox, I've read your fanfiction.
You have some real strange fans, Who write about your ring.
They know your sound! So do I want to know?
I think it may creep me out, what do you say?

Never really cared for you, I preferred Mighty.
What is your sound?
Do I even care?
this song is, this song is, this song is old!

#BADNIK Lyrics:

Hey Tails what's up.
Long time no see buddy. I'm so stressed out!
I think I'm having an identity crisis.
Green eyes, black eyes, pink arms, blue arms.
And since did I wear a neckerchief
Soooo, what do you think?
Does it makes me like a hero?
A guy who loves adventure?
Or a hipster?
I look like a hipster don't I.
I knew it.
And why don't I boost anymore. Is that too 2008?
I need to take my angst out on something, maybe prank knuckles.
That's always fun.
But first, LET ME SMASH A BADNIK

Did you see Baldy Mc Nose Hair!
He's hanging around that Princess Elise (chuckle)
He can have her
I went through my human phase.
What was I thinking?!
Eh, anyway I think I saw Eggman in the restroom.
Too many subway lunches does that.
Hey whiles he's in there,
LET ME SMASH ANOTHER BADNIK

Wait, pause, where IS Knuckles?
Is he ok?
I last saw him at the gym
He's been going a lot these days.
Too much.
Is he taking steroids?
He looks really different recently.
What even happened to the master emerald?!
Ok, I need to get going.
Uh oh, is that Marine the raccoon?
Oh wait, it's just sticks the badger.
Original character.
Do not steal.
Seriously though let's go.
My sports tape is coming off.
Can we go to a JD Sports.
Then time to smash a new BADNIK.

THE RETURN OF THE PODCAST

The Sonic Show Podcast had become a neglected child in the iTunes landscape. We had all moved on to the glorious world of on demand video from YouTube and the idea of downloading a 500 megabyte video file to then transfer on to your iPod was something nobody wanted to do anymore. Once in a while I would upload a video from the Youtube channel to the podcast feed, but it wasn't very often and nobody really cared. Once in a while we recorded discussion panels for the podcast. When the last generation of games consoles were revealed everyone hopped on Skype and we all let our opinions run free. When SEGA revealed the Sonic Boom franchise we did the same again. These recordings, which we called The Opinion Zone proved hugely popular, but for some reason it never clicked with me that something more could be made of this popularity. That was however, until I decided to do one of these recordings for the Shenmue 3 reveal at E3 2015.

The crew all got together, plus an unsuspecting Jordan aka SonicpoX, who was added to our Skype call by accident but decided not to leave and instead joined the recording. We also managed to get Fuad on to the call, a person who had not worked on the show for years. I don't know what it was, but the chemistry just worked. We decided to do further recordings, and now The Opinion Zone is a permanent fixture of The Sonic Show.

It's weird how quickly everyone settled into their roles. I get to host the show, and pretend to steer through each episode while being a little bit of a bitch. Donnie is half asleep and the butt of every joke as he never talks. Tom on the other hand is the butt of every joke because he wants to speak too much! Usually going off topic or crossing a line in decency. SonicpoX (renamed Uncle Poxxy by the show) is the loose canon who truly does not care what people think of him and what is going on. And good old Fuad is the voice of reason. Everyone has their role and the show is never the same when one person has to miss a recording.

It's also proven to be a fantastic way to interact with the fans! With people calling in, and people writing in letters for us to read, it is probably the closest we have ever been with our audience. The show has also been a big hit with the audience, placing The Sonic Show back into the top of the iTunes charts, showing that there is still life in the podcasting format we started with all those years ago.

THE CHATTY BIT
Uncle Poxxy aka SonicpoX
The Opinion Zone Co Host.

When did you first hear of The Sonic Show?
I listened and watched The Sonic Show on their podcasts many years ago on my iPod nano, watching Red Hedgehog and the Top 5's. When I found out they had a youtube channel I immediately subscribed, I have been subscribed ever since and each video brings the same level of wacky sonic-ness since the early years of the podcasts.

You are now a permanent part of the channel's roster, but how did the show find you and what led to your position now on the show?
I'm known for making Source Film Maker animations on youtube, mainly about Sonic with one that I'm usually known for being Sweet Dream (thanks for the plug Jamie x). Jamie was begging for months trying to get me into The Sonic Show; emails, youtube messages, tweets. It was insane, so after the first 500 messages I finally agreed, totally didn't accidentally get added to the opinion zone Skype chat and forced Jamie to make me stay oh god no. After that one single podcast about Shenmue 3 and Sonic Boom, Donnie decided to dub me 'Uncle Poxxy'. Why? It's Donnie, when you can make sense of that guy you come let me know. Once that happened Jamie surprised all of us with a new segment of the podcast known as Ask Uncle Poxxy, a sort of Agony Aunt column but with an uncle... on a podcast.

You've been a hit with the shows audience with things like 'Ask Uncle Poxxy'. How does it feel to be so warmly received by viewers, some who have been watching for almost a decade.
It's absolutely unbelievable, since I've been a fan of the show for years, sometimes it doesn't seem real that I'm even here, let alone people want to listen to me cuss and give horrible advice on the sexual relations of sonic characters, real nutters some of the fans are. But it's truly an honour that I can entertain people other than making animations based around the blue hedgehog, and I still can't thank Jamie enough.

You, along with Miles are part of the new generation of the show. Where can it go next?
Who knows, The Sonic Show has always been unpredictable, and I think thats how it should stay, bringing new surprises for viewers and keeping what made it so great in the first place. Miles is truly making his mark here and I hope I can do the same too. So to everyone who ever watched a top 5, a tanner LP or listened to a Podcast, I want to say personally, thank you for tuning in and thank you for accepting me into this crazy group, and I hope I can make you smile laugh and rage more in the future.

Boomin' Marvelous

Along with The Opinion Zone podcast, we also host a discussion podcast that reviews each episode of the Sonic Boom TV show. This is a counterpart with Sonic Boom Commentaries, a series hosted by Kevin Eva, Cat (doublexxcross) and the elusive Donnie. During this series, the very creative Cat has created numerous pieces of art, all from the off the wall conversations had during the show. Here are some of my personal favourites.

http://needsmoarhedgehog.tumblr.com/

Art by KatrinDarkDragon
KetrinDarkDragon.deviantart.com

The Sonic Show's 2015 Remix Lyrics

Verse 1
I can make your merchandise decrease in value,
Like how Jay Egge Man smashed Jono D's statue.
I'm a bad dude, but not as bad as Tanner who
despite all his efforts can't complete Sonic 2! (ooooh)
Who you calling an OC?
I'm an O.G, don't nobody own me.
Spindash through the snow, no time to press pause.
We're kicking down your doors with Santa the Clause!

Chorus
Ay! Yo! Ay! Yo!
Ay! Yo! Ay! Yo!
(Tune on in, Come on! Let's Go!)
Hey, yo! It's The Sonic Show
Hey, yo! It's The Sonic Show
(Tune on in, Come on! Let's GO!)

Verse 2
You rang, Chief? I'm armed and lethal.
Got my crosshairs locked on the Hedgehog Evil.
Press play, let's play, grab a snack and sit,
Off the bat, I'ma smash and hashtag a #BADNIK!
Running this channel with a Hyper-status groove.
A thick beat that gets the Intern movin'
Jono D. send Jay's base launching.
Wait, you wanna talk smack? Shut up, Donnie!

Chorus

CREDITS
Music produced and performed by Zone Runners :: http://zonerunners.net/
DiGi Valentine :: https://www.youtube.com/user/DiGiValentine
Dr. halc :: https://twitter.com/dr_halc
Sir Jordanius :: https://twitter.com/MrJordanEtienne

The YouTube Comment Section:

A study by Tanner Bachnick

When I joined The Sonic Show, I was astounded to see how many comments its videos got every minute – it was really something spectacular coming from a channel of less than 1000 subscribers at the time. I made a vow to read every comment posted that day as a means of understanding our audience more.

This might have been the worst mistake I ever made.

Comments on Sonic videos are... amazing. In that they always leave me amazed that someone wrote what they did. Before I go into it, let me just say that we do get great, funny and well thought out comments from time to time and I do love those! It just... is only about 3% of the time. It is VERY rare. The bulk of the comments fall into a couple categories:

The Sonic Lover.

Despite being, what I assume, to be a pretty fair channel with what we enjoy and don't, there's always someone who gets uppity if we say ONE THING negatively about ANY game. Even for games that are really great, any small touch of criticism makes them think we hate it outright. Of special note are the ones who defend Rise of Lyric and 06, as there really isn't much positive to say about them. Despite this, these commenters will always call us out, saying they loved the games and that we are just haters.

The Sonic Hater.
Sometimes you people straight up dissing Sonic itself and not even commenting on our videos. Or making fun of us for just making videos about Sonic. Sometimes we get told to make videos about Minecraft instead. To all of these, all I can say is that at least we're doing something productive and not spending our time commenting stuff uselessly. Neener Neener.

The Argument Crew.
Similar to The Sonic Lover, when someone else comments something negative, these people swoop in to argue. Sometimes it's civil, but most of the time it devolves into a mess of really sad swearing fits. I think these people are usually younger too, because their swears don't even make much sense in context.

Role Players.
Oh man. I won't get into it but let's just say that some comments get into the hundreds for responses that are just *blushes at @BLUEBLURSONICKU1999* or *hugs u*

Those Guys.
You know. FIRST or LOL. Please stop.

Weird Foreign Comments.
First off, I'm not knocking anyone if their first language isn't English and they watch our videos. That's awesome! Learning English is tough and I totally understand if some comments are grammatically incorrect. But like... I'm looking at a comment right now and it's just "legal". WHAT DOES THAT MEAN

Skyler Haters.
Not much to say other than that people really hate Skyler and that makes me laugh.

So yeah. There's a lot of comments that we get that are terrible or just weird, but I think that's the same for most channels of our nature. It's my fault, as I was the one who made the mistake to read all the comments, not the fault of the commenters themselves. And let it be known that for a good comment is worth 1000 bad comments, and that's why I keep reading. Thanks guys.

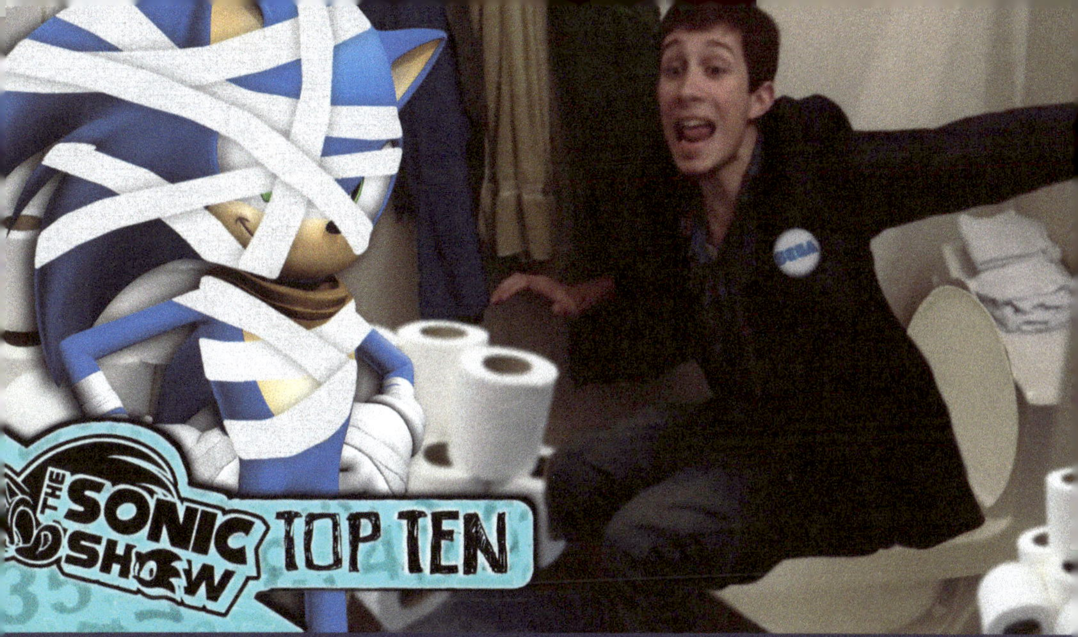
THE SONIC SHOW
TOP TEN

WTF?
THE SONIC SHOW

9590
8400
THE SONIC SHOW
PODCAST
DONNIE

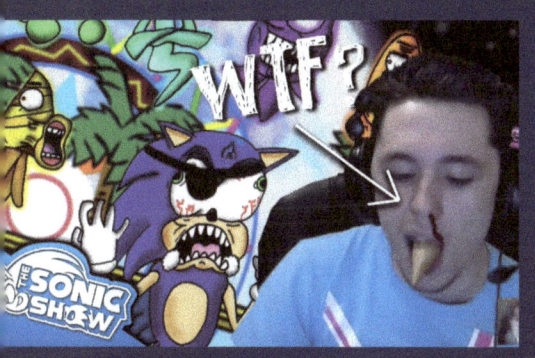

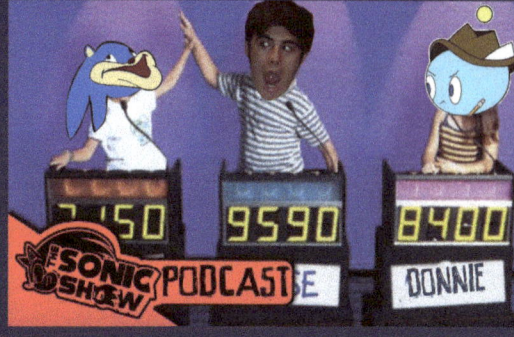

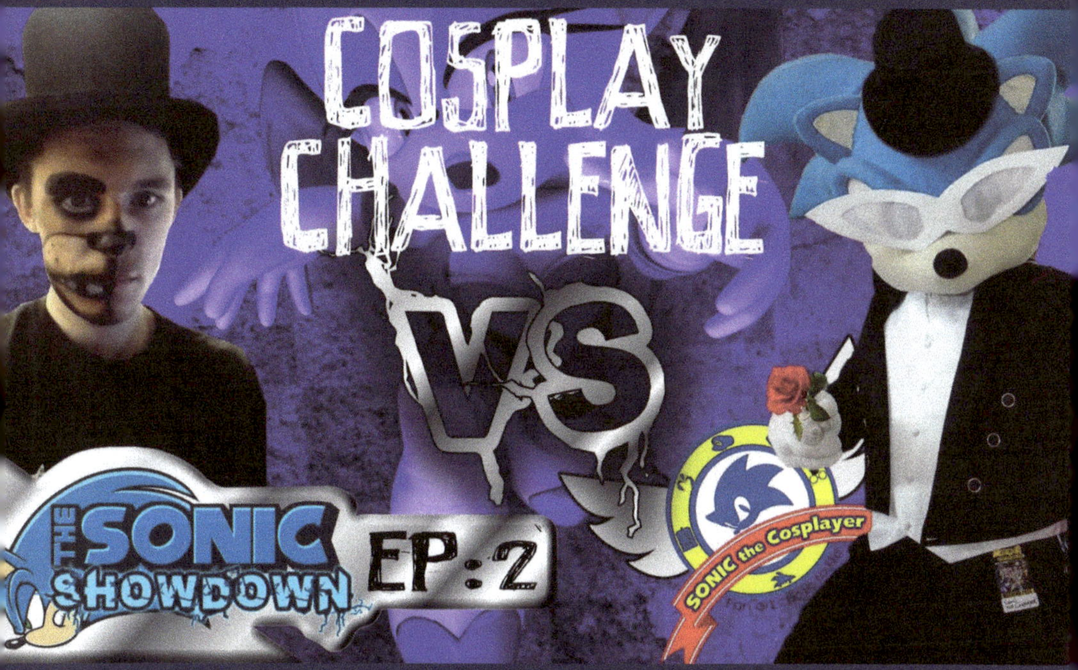
COSPLAY
CHALLENGE
VS
THE SONIC SHOWDOWN
EP:2
SONIC the Cosplayer

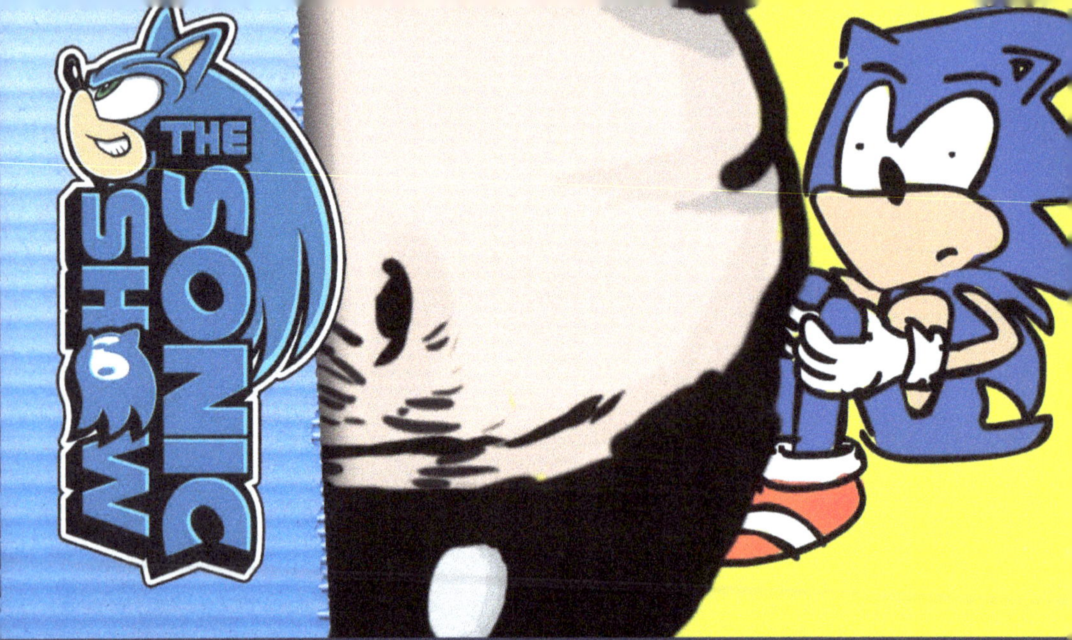
THE SONIC SHOW

THE SONIC SHOW
LET'S PLAY

SONIC
UNFAIR
VS
THE SONIC SHOWDOWN
EP:1

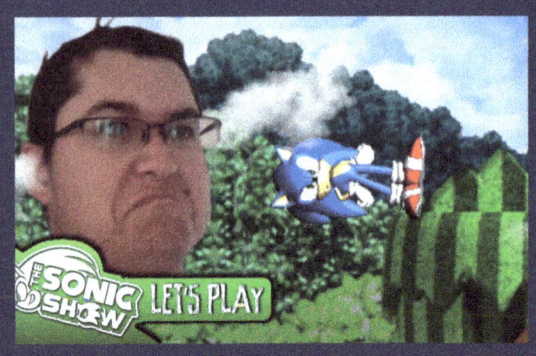

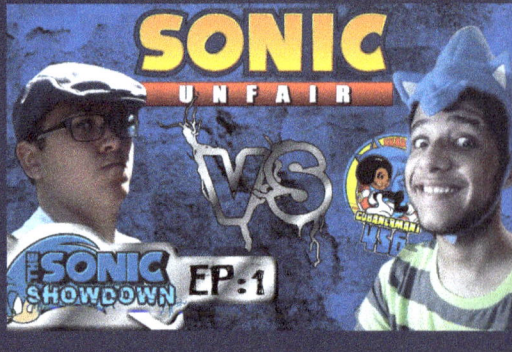

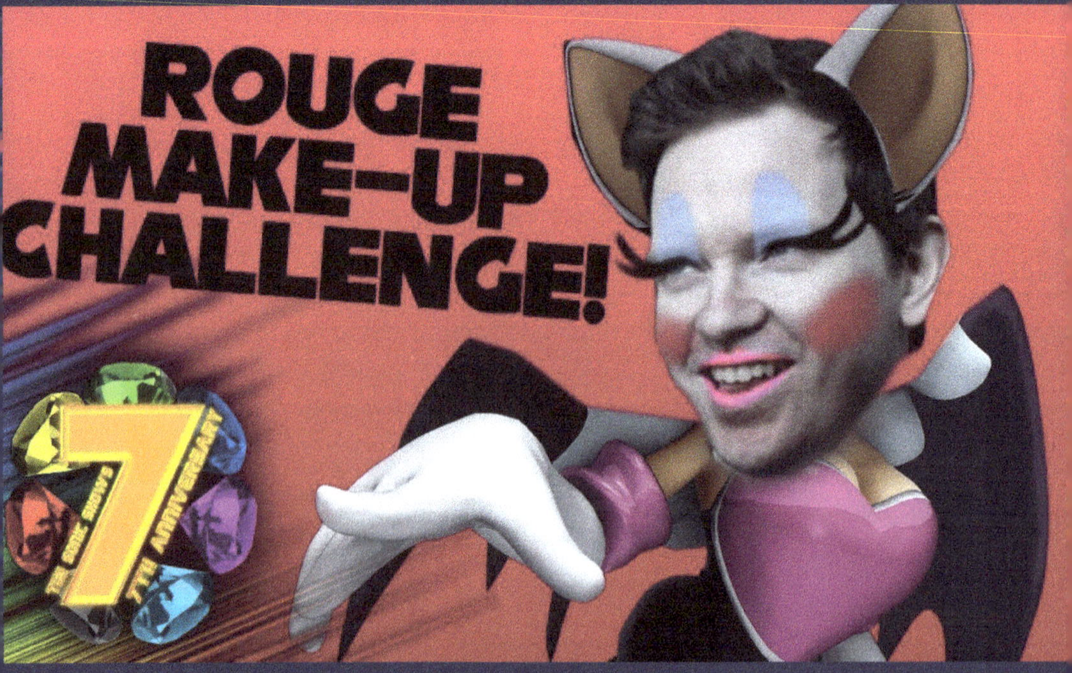
ROUGE MAKE-UP CHALLENGE!
7
THE SONIC SHOW'S 7TH ANNIVERSARY

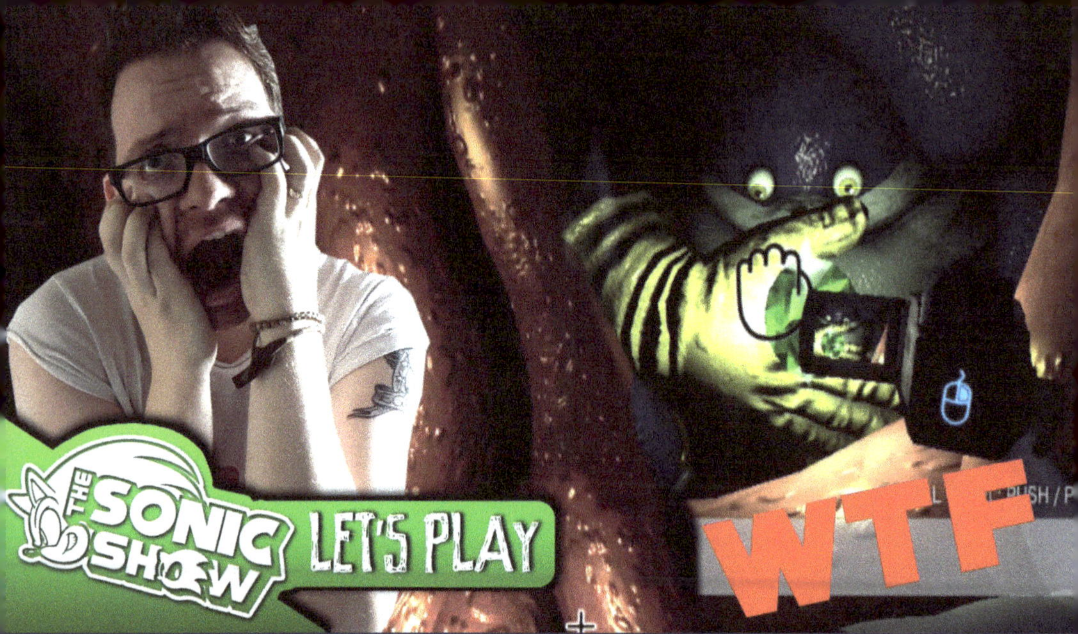
THE SONIC SHOW
LET'S PLAY
WTF

I'll keep a tab on this so i don't forget.
Not long now!

TOP TEN EASTER EGGS
THE SONIC SHOW
TOP 10

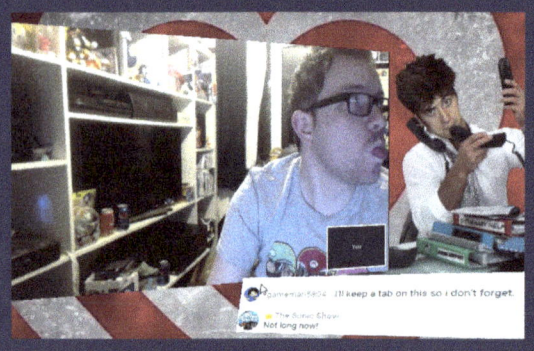

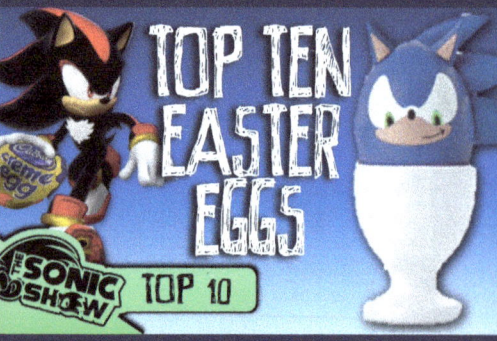

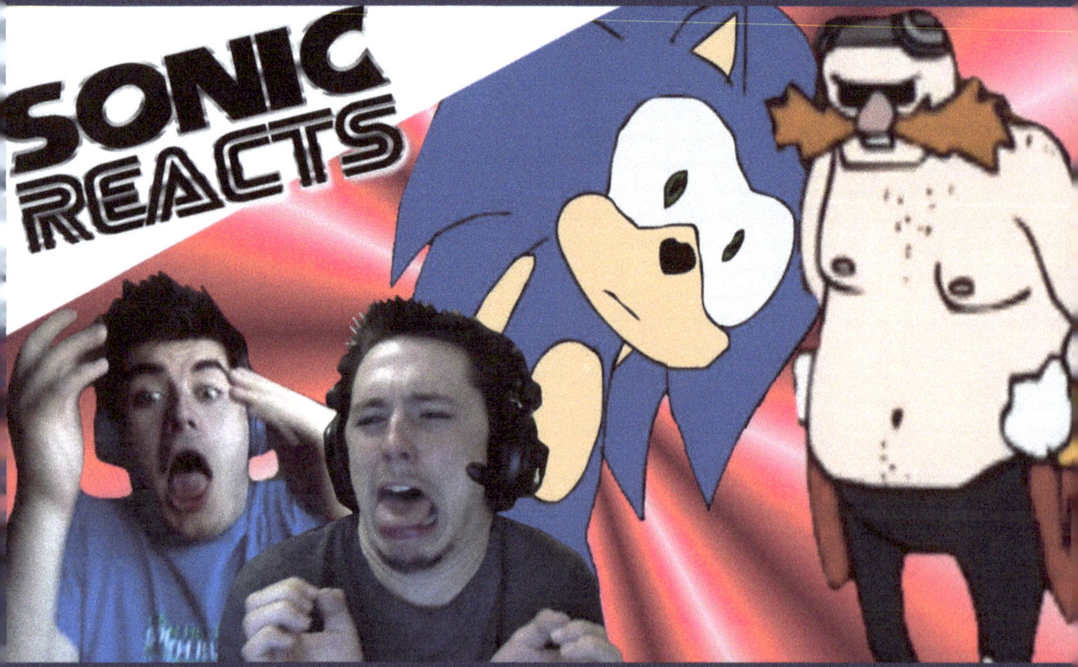
SONIC REACTS

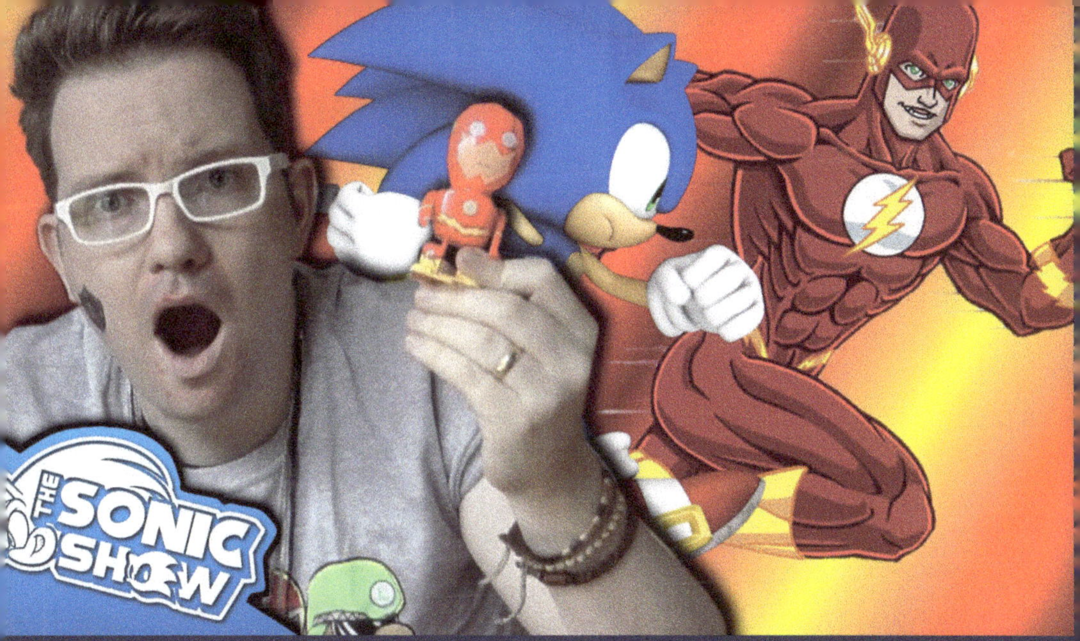
THE SONIC SHOW

MIKE'S ALL ABOUT THAT BASS
THE SONIC SHOW

THE SONIC SHOW TOP FIVE
sonic in twilight

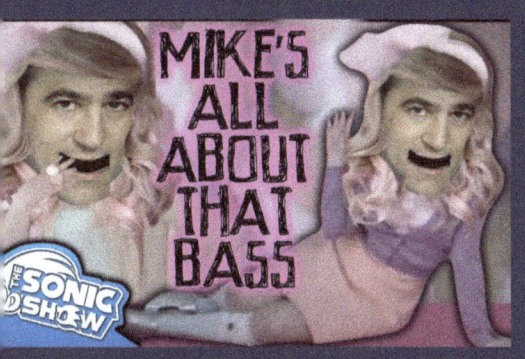

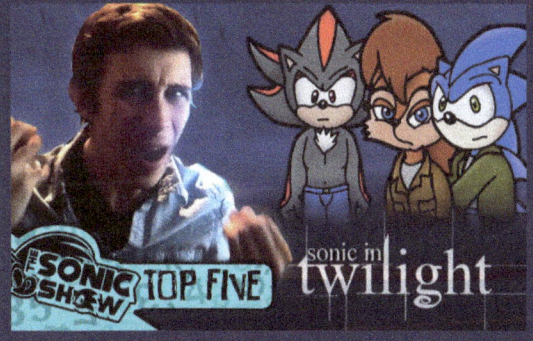

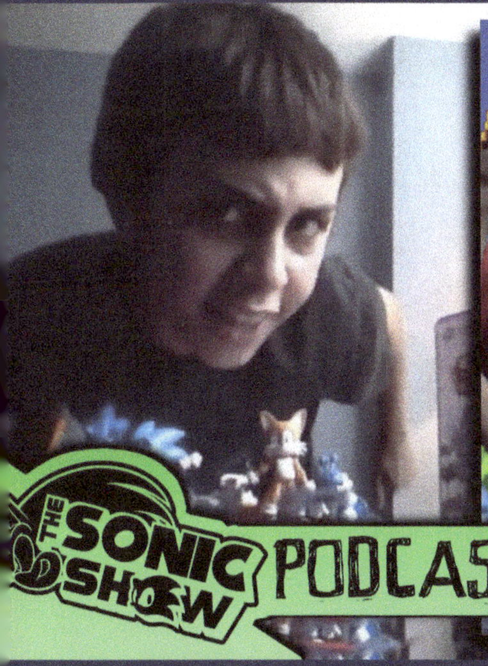
THE SONIC SHOW PODCAST

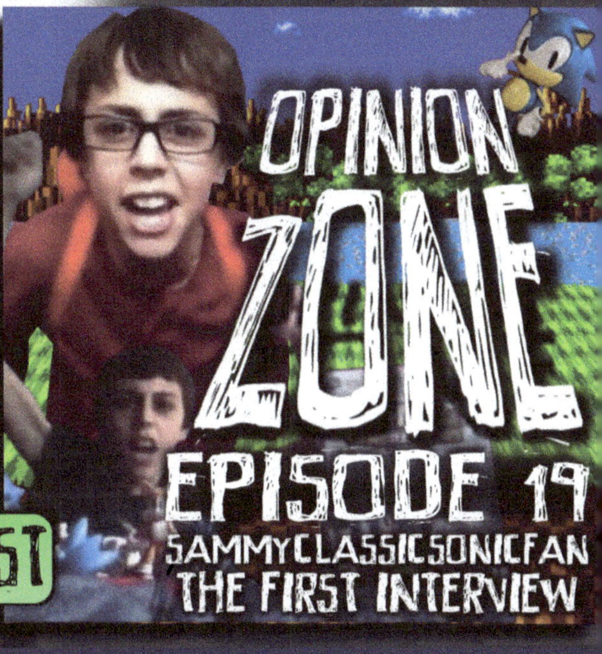
OPINION ZONE
EPISODE 19
SAMMYCLASSICSONICFAN
THE FIRST INTERVIEW

SO, WHAT'S NEXT?

What awaits for the future of The Sonic Show? Honestly, that is a much harder question to answer than you would think.

I am so proud of what we have done. But I will not pretend that it is easy to keep finding ways to make things interesting this far in to a show's timeline. Next year will mark ten years of The Sonic Show, which I feel will be a turning point for the show. Right up until now I have tried so hard to stay relevant. Trying to keep up with what is trending and cool in the internet landscape, to be honest, is not always fun. I think after our tenth year, the way I view the show will change. It is going to have to change

I am now creeping into my thirties and the reality is life gets in the way. Do I want to keep up with what the "young ones" are doing? They have already surpassed us in popularity so maybe it is time to accept that we are getting old.

So what does that mean for the future? Well, I feel what the show creates will reflect more on what I find fun to do. The reason I brought The Opinion Zone podcast to life was because it is a chance to have fun with my friends. Unlike other channels who chase subscribers, beg you to follow them on Vine, or ask you to turn on upload notifications, maybe I will just do what amuses me and if people want to join in, well that's awesome. I think the novelty of chasing new fans is fading. Before it was about getting the highest number of viewers. That is all I wanted. I needed it to validate myself. It proved I was worth something. Looking back now I can see that wasn't what was important.

Does the millions of views and millions of downloads mean something to me? Of course they do, but you know what really means the more to me? Meeting, getting to know and becoming friends with people who I looked up to when I first found the internet community. People like Svend Joscelyne, Kevin Eva and Adam Tuff. Trusting people to help me make content for The Sonic Show, like Tanner, Tom, Jono D, Donnie (I guess) and Uncle Poxxy, all who I now consider a close group of friends. Feeling part of a family at Summer Of Sonic with all the people who worked at the events. Having people who enjoy the show that I recognise, people who have been around for years. Yeah, that's what means the most to me from making this strange show over the years.

Next year will be a great year for myself and the team. Screw 25 years of Sonic, 2016 is the year to celebrate The Sonic Show. Ten years is a huge achievement for any fan project, so we are going to milk it to death! There should never be any shame in lasting this long in the community! We have stuck it through things like Sonic holding a sword drama, Sonic 4 leaking drama and do not get me started on what happened to Sonic Boom: Rise of Lyric! We have lost friends and made friends. And somehow it just keeps on going. Maybe because I don't have the guts to end it, but more so because I don't think I could imagine life without this show!

I guess I should thank you for taking the time to skim through these pages. This is more of a glorified pamphlet than a book, but hopefully you were able to appreciate it for what it was meant to be. A nice little way to archive what this show was and what it has become before we wrap up our first ten years of stupidity.

So here is to another decade of this shambles of random creativity. A precious hug to everyone who has been involved in one way or another along the journey to this point. And a huge warm welcome to all the new people we will meet going forward on the road to glorious and wonderful mediocrity.

Oh, and shut up Donnie.

See you next year...

Index and Sources

Cat aka doublexxcross (42)	http://needsmoarhedgehog.tumblr.com/
Chris Light aka Christopher James (32)	https://soundcloud.com/chrislight-2
Donnie aka SSF1991 (40, 41, 42, 55)	https://twitter.com/SSF1991
Fuad (40, 41)	https://www.youtube.com/channel/UCbJUAnOJjlOrIbRkJI-r_0A
Hunter Bridges (18)	https://soundcloud.com/hunterbridges/
Josiah Haworth aka Legend20X (20)	http://legend20x.deviantart.com/
Kevin Eva aka ArchangelUK (21)	http://lastminutecontinue.com/
Last Minute Continue (21, 42)	http://lastminutecontinue.com/
Lewis Clark aka Sonic Yoda (38)	https://twitter.com/sonicyoda
Matthew Walker (33)	http://matthewwalker1.bandcamp.com/
Nick Kalmer aka PiggyBank aka MarkandFlops (30, 31)	https://www.youtube.com/user/MarkandFlops
Professor J (15, 16, 17, 19, 30)	http://professor-j.deviantart.com/
Red Panda Audio (32, 33)	http://www.redpandaaudio.com/
Sega Driven (38)	http://www.segadriven.com/
Slingerland (13)	https://info.sonicretro.org/Slingerland
Sonic Cage Dome (7)	http://soniccagedome.com/home/
SonicpoX aka Uncle Poxxy (40, 41, 44)	https://www.youtube.com/user/Sonicpox
Sonic Wrecks (11, 21)	https://twitter.com/sonicwrecks
Summer Of Sonic (34, 35)	http://summerofsonic.com
Svend Joscelyne (14)	https://twitter.com/SvendJoscelyne
Tanner Bachnick (28, 29, 46, 47)	https://www.youtube.com/user/goodbye18000
The Opinion Zone (40, 41)	http://thesonicshow.org/theopinionzone
The Sonic Stadium (12)	http://thesonicstadium.org
Todd Hakusho (10)	
Tom aka LunaEC64 (40, 41)	https://twitter.com/LunaEC64
TSSZ News (26)	http://www.tssznews.com/
VGM:Awesome (32, 33)	https://www.facebook.com/vgmawesome/
Weston Super Sonic (34)	http://westonsupersonic.wix.com/weston-super-sonic
Zone Runners (45)	http://zonerunners.net/

Credits

Written and designed by Jay Egge Mann..
Contributions from Tanner Bachnick, Jordan Rutter, Todd Hakusho, Svend Joscelyne, Christopher James and Matthew Walker.
Edited by Megan Williams

www.ingramcontent.com/pod-product-compliance
Lightning Source LLC
Chambersburg PA
CBHW040110180526
45172CB00009B/1290